The  Inside of ME.

by Shanicka Vail
Illustrated by Lauren Lacy

The "i" Inside of ME.

Shanicka Vail
Copyright Info

Book design by Lauren Lacy, Miss Lacy Studios

First Edition

This book is dedicated to my Grandmother,
Ruth Mae Cobbs Vail.

...and to every girl who, through this,
will be introduced to the greater her!!

Ye are of God, little children, and have
overcome them: because greater is he that is in you,
than he that is in the world. (1 John 4:4 KJV)

- i.Am LOVED

I am accepted for the little Princess that I am,
and for the be.Utee qUeen I'll one day grow
to be.
I will not question how much I am loved
and cared
for… I know that I am here
because Someone AMAZING loves me!

- **i.Am NICE**

I say "HI" when I pass someone on the street…
Or when an elderly person walks in the room,
I offer them my seat…
I lend a smile, a hand, and even a hug…
Because "nice-ness" is what
the world could use a lot more of.

- i.Am GIVING

It is better to give than to receive…
So I come up with ways to help those
in need…
I might not have money, but I
do have some time… and it doesn't cost
me anything to just be.Kind.

- i.Am OBEDIENT

I follow directions and abide by the rules…
I don't have a problem doing as I'm instructed
to do…
I am given the
FREEDOM to be me, but given guidelines
to use as tools…
to help me be the BEST ME I can be, and
let the love of
obedience shine through.

- i.Am SMART

I always do my very best…
I study hard to pass each test…
I give 100%, and nothing less…
because a princess
works in EXCELLENCE!

- i.Am NEAT

I look my best, and I smell SOOO sweet,
because I always practice good hygiene…
I am well put together and it
doesn't cost me much, just the time it takes
to 'keep it up'.
You can look nice without spending ALL that
you have,
just spend the time it takes to make it
LOOK FAB!

- i.Am CREATIVE

I can write a song, and even a book…
I can make up a dance that makes
everyone look!
My artwork should be framed, and my
inventions
should be sold… Because the things that
I create are truly valuable!

- i.Am GIFTED

I won't judge myself by the things that you can do…
Because your gifts are YOURS, so they make room for YOU! I have talents of my own, they're my own special gifts to use…
Let's just work them together, as a team… and that way we can't lose!

- i.Am BEAUTIFUL

The curl of my hair,
the tint of my skin,
the sparkle in my eye,
the warmth in my grin…
Those are the things that make me PRETTY,
you see…
but what makes me BEAUTIFUL
lies inside of me!

- i.Am BRAVE

There is nothing to fear,
not even fear itself…
Because I can do ALL things with my
Father's help… I won't run and hide
even when that seems to be right…
I'll stand firm, square my shoulders,
and fight, Fight, FIGHT!

• i.Am ROYALTY

I don't think that I am any better than you…
I just think highly of myself,
and you should too… I don't look down
on anyone, because God loves us all…
I just walk with my head held high
so that my crown doesn't fall.

- i.Am UNIQUE

I'm number ONE at being myself…
I'll never be number two…
because I was made to be ME, and you were
made to be.U! I am one of a kind,
there's no one else on earth just like me…
because i.Am NOT a carbon copy of any
other Princess – i.Am UNIQUE!!!!!!!!!!

TO CONTACT THE AUTHOR

- Email: admin@anchoredroyalty.com
&
anchoredroyalty@gmail.com
- Instagram: @shanickavail
- Twitter: @shanickavail
- Facebook: Shanicka Vail

Made in the USA
Lexington, KY
16 December 2014